Happiness
And Other Life Seasonings

Happiness
And Other Life Seasonings

Cathy Burnham Martin

Published and printed in the United States of America

QUIET THUNDER

www.QTPublishing.com

Quiet Thunder Publishing
Naples, FL   Manchester, NH   Columbus, NC

**This title and more can be found at
www.GoodLiving123.com**

Paperback edition: ISBN 978-1-939220-69-1
eBook edition: ISBN 978-1-939220-70-7
Audiobook edition: ISBN 978-1-939220-71-4

Library of Congress Control Number: 2025915413

Dedication

I dedicate "Happiness: and Other Life Seasonings" to my late father, Robert Burnham. When I was a scrappy kid, my emotions tended to run to extremes. Dad often noted that when I was "up," no one could be any higher, but when I was "down," no one could be any lower either. He tried to guide me with the example of a swinging pendulum, assuring me that I would be a much happier person if I could learn to moderate my emotional swings closer to the middle.

Of course, the rebellious child in me did not want a parent to be correct. But, as usual, he was right.

Thus, from personal experience, I know we can work to grow ourselves into more balanced, compassionate, and positively happy people. And I believe we can truly radiate a zest for life and exude a healthy sense of calmness, even in challenging times.

Thanks, Dad… again… for teaching me and guiding me along a path to true happiness.

Cathy

(Photo by Aleksandra Sapozhnikova)

Foreword

"Don't worry. Be happy." American singer, songwriter and conductor Bobby McFerrin (1950 -) wrote the lyrics to that delightful song not knowing that it would skyrocket to become the first a cappella song to reach number one on the Billboard Hot 100 chart.

Hearing his delightful words and playfully engaging delivery style brings a smile to people's faces, even if we were not in a good mood initially. Being happy is sought by everyone, even after the end of a gleeful song.

(Photo by Tim Mossholder)

As part of my ongoing research in life, I continually seek out and collect quips, quotations, words of wisdom, serious thoughts, and humorous tidbits. These "Notable Quotables" hail from all walks of life, the famous and the lesser known, both modern and classically aged. I share some of these gems in the Life Seasonings series of little guides to add sparkle to our thinking and support in times when harmony is deeply needed.

Understanding happiness and weaving it into the fiber of our being helps us live better, fuller lives. Being happy is a skill we can all learn. Happiness is a sweet Life Seasoning that helps us cook up ways to make good living as easy as 1-2-3.

"Happiness depends on ourselves."

-- Aristotle (384 BC – 322 BC)
Ancient Greek philosopher & polymath

Table of Contents

(Photo by Andrew Bui)

1

<u>Defining Happiness</u>

For thousands of years, countless philosophers, psychologists, and many other types of experts have struggled to define happiness. Perhaps the most precious of Life's seasonings, happiness almost defies definition. We can spin a line by Dale Carnegie into "Happiness is not having what you want but wanting what you have."

"Success is getting what you want.
Happiness is wanting what you get."

-- Dale Carnegie (1888 – 1955)
American writer & public speaking teacher

(Photo by Osman Firat)

We know that happiness is a state of well-being. People also agree that happiness is characterized by positive emotions. Words like joy, contentment, and satisfaction tend to be in everyone's descriptions. Well, perhaps not in everyone's.

> *"All you need for happiness is a good gun,*
> *a good horse, and a good wife."*

-- Daniel Boone (1734 – 1820)
American pioneer & frontiersman

Oxford and Cambridge English dictionaries agree that happiness is "the state of being happy." Well, okay, but that answers nothing.

Mirriam-Webster goes further to define happiness as a "state of well-being and contentment." Some sources reference the feeling of joy.

(Photo by Mi Pham)

Numerous studies deliver results with variations of similar lists of happiness identifiers, tenants, secrets, or pillars. Common words and phrases include bliss, smiling, cheerfulness, relationships, contentment, living in the present, optimism, and purpose. These are not defining words, but they appear more frequently as common factors that help us enjoy more happiness.

(Photo by Greg Rakozy)

"Happiness is when what you think, what you say, and what you do are in harmony."

-- Mahatma Gandhi (1869 - 1948)
Indian lawyer and political ethicist

Regardless of how we choose to define it, happiness is multi-faceted and reflects a wide range of positive feelings. Further, there is no doubt that happiness revolves around flourishing and a positive state of well-being.

(Photo by Stephanie Pratt)

*"True happiness is...
to enjoy the present, without anxious
dependence upon the future."*

-- Lucius Annaeus Seneca (4 BC – 65 AD)
Ancient Roman Stoic philosopher

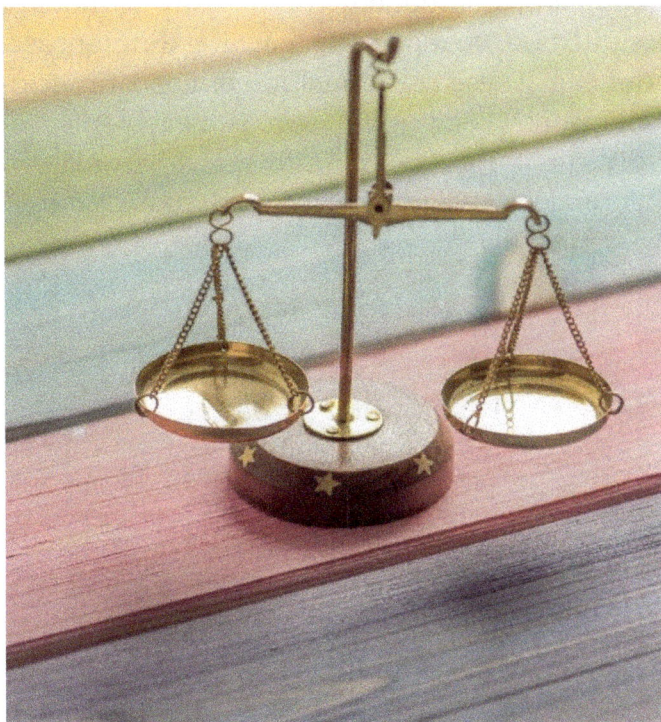

(Photo by Elena Mozhvilo)

A balance of emotions is natural, which means ups and downs, including both positive and negative emotions, feelings, and moods. Naturally, happy people likely experience more positive feelings than negative ones.

"The first recipe for happiness is: avoid too lengthy meditation on the past."

-- André Maurois (1885 – 1967)
French author

Another key component could easily be noted as how satisfied we may feel regarding different areas of our life. These could include our most precious relationships, our jobs, our achievements, our involvement in our community or church, and other aspects of living that we consider to be important.

> *"Happiness is a how; not a what.*
> *A talent, not an object."*
>
> -- Hermann Hesse (1877 – 1962)
> German-Swiss poet & novelist

(Photo by Johan Godinez)

When positive emotions like joy, contentment, and satisfaction surround us, we can more readily recognize that our life is good. Also, we all need to feel meaningful and worthwhile. These are very different things to different people, and that is fine. We all have different life circumstances, and we have to work within our comfort zones to develop a sense of purpose and fulfillment in life.

"There is something curiously boring about somebody else's happiness."

-- Aldous Huxley (1894 – 1963)
English writer & philosopher

(Photo by Noah Silliman)

Happiness does not mean that we are constantly euphoric. Instead, despite ups and downs in our lives, we can develop a mindset to experience more positive than negative. We are building our happiness foundation.

We need more than a good mood to be happy. We need deep contentment and a sense of meaning.

(Photo by Priscilla duPreez)

"Happiness is spiritual, born of truth and love. It is unselfish; therefore, it cannot exist alone but requires all mankind to share it."

-- Mary Baker Eddy (1821 – 1910)
American religious leader & author
Founder of the Church of Christ

2

Happiness Types

There are many different ways of thinking about happiness. For example, the ancient Greek philosopher Aristotle believed that one type of happiness was Eudaimonia. This type is achieved by living a life filled with self-improvement and virtuous actions. The focus is more on long-term goals and focusing on helping other people. To live up to personal ideals, Aristotle also emphasized taking personal responsibility in attaining happiness.

"Happiness depends on ourselves."

-- Aristotle (384 BC – 322 BC)
Ancient Greek philosopher & polymath

The ancient philosopher also suggested that there were four levels of happiness. He believed it starts at the lowest level, where we receive immediate gratification. Then happiness is found via comparison and achievement. Happiness grows fuller by making positive contributions. And the top level of happiness blossoms when we achieve fulfillment in life.

(Photo by Gerd Altmann)

"Action may not always bring happiness; but there is no happiness without action."

-- Benjamin Disraeli (1804 – 1881)
British statesman &
Prime Minister of the United Kingdom

Today's leading psychological experts also draw distinctions in types of happiness. They refer to Hedonia, which indicates pleasure and a lack of distress. As noted, a second type of happiness is Eudemonia, which involves deeper meaning and a sense of flourishing. Some experts also consider a third type of happiness, which occurs when we actively participate in or engage positively with life.

*"Most of us believe in
trying to make other people happy
only if they can be happy
in ways which we approve."*

-- Robert Staughton Lynd (1892 – 1970)
American sociologist & professor

Pleasure, involvement, and deeper meaning will also be different for each of us. We may enjoy some activities that are only pleasurable and meaningful to us, personally. These activities could include active involvement with others in our communities, families, church organizations, or employment areas.

(Photo by Ahmet Kurt)

For example, many people take great pleasure in helping out in a worthwhile cause. This also includes engaging with others and usually carries great meaning and value in our lives. On the other hand, some people might not find any pleasure at all in volunteering personal time for committees or programs, regardless of the "cause."

"The way I see it,
if you want the rainbow,
you gotta
put up with the rain!"
-- Dolly Parton (1946 -)
American singer, songwriter, actress,
& philanthropist

(Photo by Mateus Campos Felipe)

"Happiness is a butterfly,
which when pursued,
is always just beyond your grasp,
but which, if you will sit down quietly,
may alight upon you."

-- Nathaniel Hawthorne (1804 – 1864)
American novelist

(Photo by Suzanne D. Williams)

"For me, the opposite of happiness isn't sadness but boredom."

-- Sushant Singh Rajput (1986 – 2020)
Indian actor

"You can be happy where you are."

-- Joel Osteen (1963 -)
American pastor & televangelist

Many people like kicking back in the evenings to watch a favorite TV program. Perhaps this is high on a personal pleasure scale, but it likely ranks low on a scale measuring meaningful happiness. For someone else, watching television may not bring even superficial pleasure, never mind meaningful happiness.

*"It is neither wealth nor splendor;
but tranquility and occupation
which give you happiness."*

-- Thomas Jefferson (1743 – 1826)
American Founding Father,
3rd President of the United States, &
Author of the Declaration of Independence

A family gathering may be high on a meaningful scale. However, if there are issues like relationship challenges, an individual's politeness should not be confused with joy, because they are not having fun at all.

(Photo by Aizhan Okisheva)

"If you wait for the perfect moment
when all is safe and assured,
it may never arrive.
Mountains will not be climbed,
races won,
or lasting happiness achieved."

-- Maurice Chevalier (1888 – 1972)
French singer & actor

Regardless of the type of happiness or any specific definition, feelings and emotions become big parts of our happiness. From momentary joy, positive anticipation, or excitement to gratitude, pride in an accomplishment, contentment, or an optimistic outlook, happiness brings a sense of satisfaction.

"It is in the compelling zest
of high adventure and of victory,
and in creative action,
that man finds his supreme joys."

-- Antoine de Saint-Exupery (1900 – 1944)
French writer

"*All animals, except man, know that the principal business of life is to enjoy it.*"
-- Samuel Butler (1835 – 1902)
English novelist & critic

(Photo by Daria Shatova)

3

<u>Happiness Is Not</u>

Happiness does not mean we are in some constantly euphoric state. That is unreasonable to expect. Very happy people feel negative emotions in their full range of experiences. To be happy, however, we must not let negative emotions bog us down.

*"You cannot
protect yourself from sadness
without
protecting yourself from happiness."*

-- Jonathan Safran Foer (1977 -)
American novelist

Happiness is not a world completely void of anger, frustration, boredom, loneliness, or sadness. However, happiness is also not a world that lets discomfort overload an optimistic foundation. We must be confident that we will be able to feel happy again, even if balance becomes more difficult to maintain.

(Photo by Kyle Loftus)

*"The happiness of most people is
not ruined by great catastrophes or fatal errors,
but by the repetition of
slowly destructive little things."*

-- Ernest Dimnet (1866 – 1954)
French priest & writer

Happiness is not the same thing to all people. Further, our happiness will vary between places, times of the day, and stages of our lives.

*"The two enemies of human happiness
are pain and boredom."*

-- Arthur Schopenhauer (1788 – 1860)
German philosopher

Happiness is not objective. Someone says, "Oh, you should be happy!" Well, that is not necessarily true. Happiness is subjective. It is personal. What makes one person happy may not make someone else happy.

Happiness is not just the absence of negativity. Happiness needs a positive state of mind.

*"Happiness is inward, and not outward;
and so, it does not depend on what we have,
but on what we are."*

-- Henry Van Dyke (1852 – 1933)
American author, educator, diplomat &
Presbyterian clergyman

(Photo by Mark Adriane)

Happiness does not happen in negative isolation, regardless of how positive-minded we may be. This is not to say that we cannot be happy when we are alone.

Being alone, however, is not the same as feeling isolated. Being alone can be happy and restful and filled with contentment. Feeling isolated can be bleak, scary, and detrimental to both our physical and our mental health.

"Happiness is a direction, not a place."

-- Sydney J. Harris (1917 – 1986)
American journalist

(Photo by Herbert Bieser)

Happiness is not dependent on material possessions. While goods and material wealth can bring comfort and pleasure, they are not necessary for happiness. Positive experiences, relationships, and personal growth are all examples of sources of happiness that have nothing to do with material possessions.

"Procrastination is one of the most common and deadliest of diseases and its toll on success and happiness is heavy."

-- Wayne Gretzky (1961 -)
Canadian professional hockey player & coach

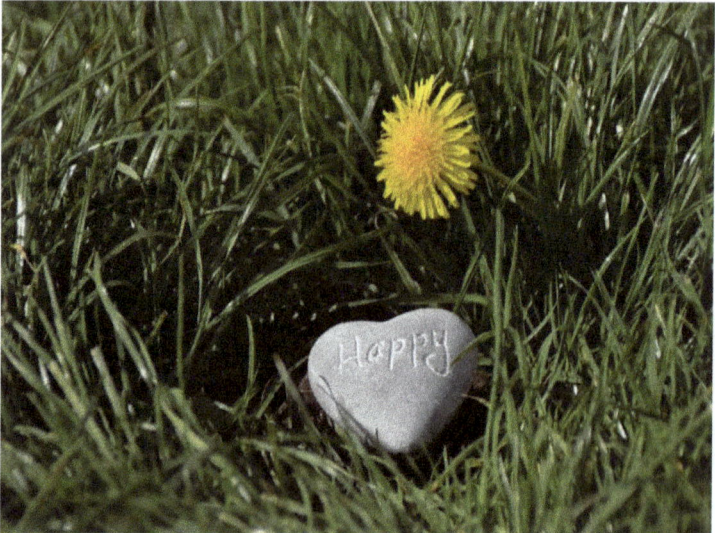

(Photo by Szilvia Basso)

Happiness is also not an imbalance of negativity over positivity. We can't rant and rave negative thoughts and words or keep hounding people or even ourselves over anything and expect to be happy. We need balance.

"Remember this, that very little is needed to make a happy life."

-- Marcus Aurelius (121 - 180 AD)
Roman Emperor & Stoic philosopher

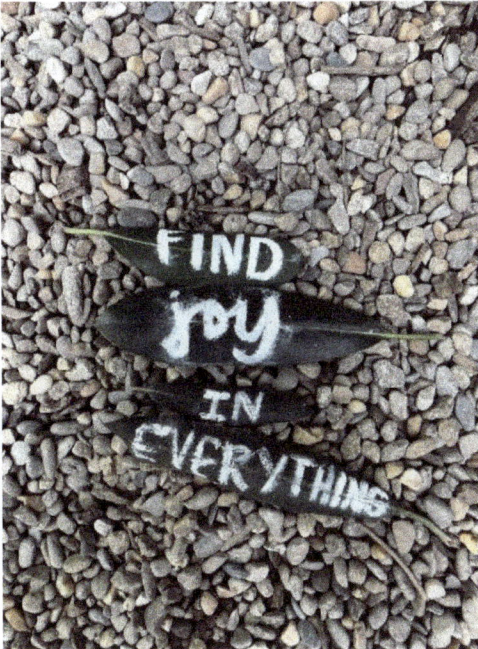

(Photo by Taylor Heery)

*"The Constitution only gives people
the right to pursue happiness.
You have to catch up with it yourself."*

-- Benjamin Franklin (1706 – 1790)
American writer, polymath, diplomat & statesman
US Founding Father &
Signer of the Declaration of Independence

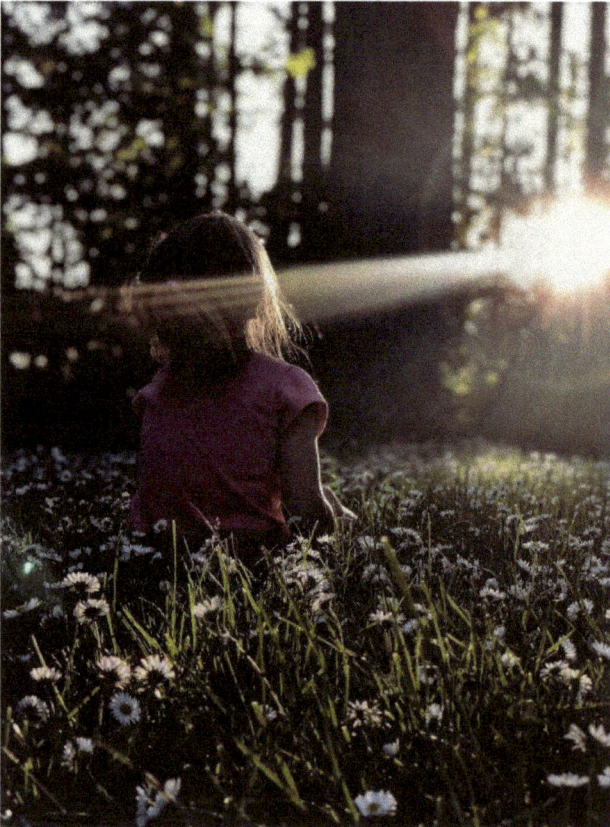

(Photo by Melissa Askew)

4

<u>More Than a Feeling</u>

Happiness can be viewed as a combination of positive emotions along with a sense of meaning, belonging, or purpose in life. However, its complexity goes well beyond feelings.

"Anything you're good at contributes to happiness."

-- Bertrand Russell (1872 – 1970)
British philosopher & logician

Thinking beyond emotion, we find that happiness is a multifaceted concept that powerfully impacts our health. Being happy is supported by making healthy choices. If we want to be happier people, we need to be healthier people… in every way.

"The groundwork of all happiness is health."

-- Leigh Hunt (1784 – 1859)
English critic & essayist

Physical Health

We all do better when we have enough sleep, good nutrition, and regular exercise. Simply taking a walk around the block is a great boost.

(Photo by Caju Gomes)

When we are happy, endorphins are released. This has an added benefit because it can reduce our feeling of physical pain and become a sort of natural painkiller.

When we are physically healthier, our immune system is boosted. Everyone wants to be more resilient to illness. We all want healthy hearts, too. Most of us can benefit from lowering our blood pressure or heart rate. Just imagine if truly being happier could lower our risk of cardiovascular disease. Studies have shown that happier people tend to live longer, healthier lives.

> *"A joyful heart is like the sunshine of God's love, the hope of eternal happiness."*

-- Mother Teresa (1910 - 1997)
Albanian Indian Catholic num & saint

(Photo by Ricardo Moura)

Mental Health

Improved mental well-being also builds up our resilience. Cognitive health helps us have stronger social connections.

Happy people tend to have stronger social connections. When we have cognitive, intellectual health, happiness is boosted.

(Photo by Tim Mossholder)

*"The way you think,
the way you behave, the way you eat,
can influence your life by 30 to 50 years."*

-- Deepak Chopra (1946 -)
Indian - American author & new age guru

When our mental health is balanced with happiness, we can cope better with the inevitable stress that life brings. We all want to be able to deal with adversity and challenges more calmly and effectively.

(Photo by Dimitris Vetsikas)

Would we like to reduce stress levels? Most of us would. A lovely fact is that positive emotions, like happiness, promote calmness and well-being. When we learn to embrace a sense of calmness, we are learning to lower anxiety.

Enhanced self-esteem is another super mental health boost that happiness delivers. A very healthy happiness side-effect is a more positive self-image.

"Eternal principles that govern happiness apply equally to all."

-- Russell M. Nelson (1924 -)
American religious leader & retired surgeon
President of the Church of
Jesus Christ of Latter-Day Saints

Social Health

When we are happy, we relate better with other people. When our interactions are positive and healthy, we build stronger, more meaningful relationships.

(Photo by Tran Huynh)

Our social networks tend to be better, because we seek out positive, supportive avenues. These can prove to be valuable parts of our support system when we face challenges.

"Our greatest happiness
does not depend on the condition of life
in which chance has placed us,
but is always the result of a good conscience,
good health, occupation,
and freedom in all just pursuits."

-- Thomas Jefferson (1743 – 1826)
American Founding Father; 3rd President of the
United States
Author of the Declaration of Independence

When we have positive social health, we also tend to have better empathy for other people. Compassion leads to better interactions with everyone in our lives.

Productive Health
_____

We all feel happier when we are able to focus and concentrate better. This leads to us enjoying increased productivity, which further boosts our happiness.

"A good laugh and a long sleep are the best cures in the doctor's book."

– Irish proverb

When we are productive, our creativity is boosted. We feel stimulated. This helps us view situations with confidence and fresh perspectives, increasing our coping abilities.

This also makes us more optimistic in our daily lives. When we are happy, we are more able to approach problem solving in effective ways. We become more innovative.

Mindful Health

When happy, we are more mindful or aware. This gives us a greater sense of purpose in life and can lead to a longer, more fulfilling life.

"Happiness is itself a kind of gratitude."

-- Joseph Wood Krutch (1893 – 1970)
American author

Feeling happy increases meaning in our lives. When we find things to be more meaningful, we are naturally happier overall. When we are mindful of others, we also are more in tune with contributing to the lives of others.

(Photo by Kyle Loftus)

Having more appreciation in Life helps us enjoy even the simplest joys. This is like stopping to smell the roses along the path. They may be there every day, but we sometimes forget to pay attention. When we are mindful, our awareness lets us experience life in more positive ways.

"I have chosen to be happy because it is good for my health."

-- Voltaire (1694 - 1778)
French writer & philosopher

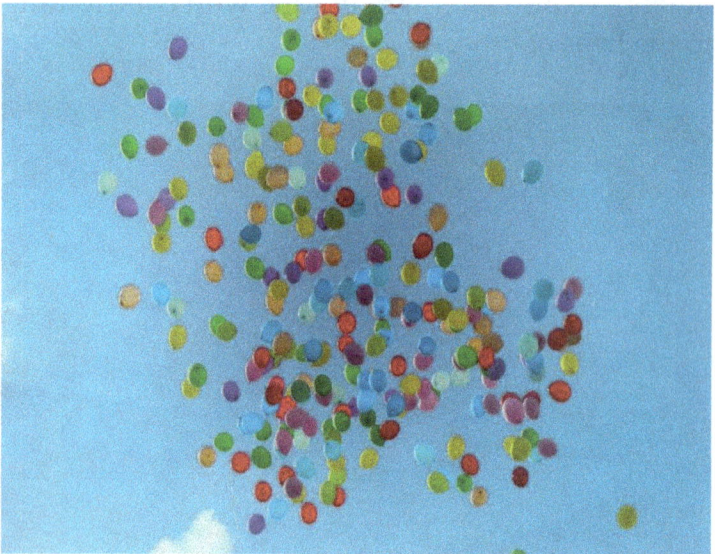

(Photo by Luca Upper)

5

Capturing the Elusive

"The pleasure which we most rarely experience gives us greatest delight."

-- Epictetus (50 - 135 AD)
Greek philosopher

Unfortunately, happiness can seem very elusive, but this does not have to remain so. We can simplify and personalize some basic concepts and develop a deep state of well-being to be able to truly enjoy a good life filled with meaning and genuine contentment.

"It is not easy to find happiness in ourselves, and it is not possible to find it elsewhere."

-- Agnes Repplier (1900 – 1944)
American essayist

Practicing gratitude and consciously being aware or mindful make big differences in our long-term happiness and overall well-being. Engaging in positive relationships is another active step to honest, identifiable happiness.

"If you want others to be happy, practice compassion. If you want to be happy, practice compassion."

-- Dalai Lama – 14th is Tenzih Gyatso (1935 -)
Spiritual leader of Tibetan Buddhism

(Photo by Kenny Eliason)

We all want happiness to be easy and a natural part of our lives. Making happiness understandable also makes it obtainable and elusive no more.

"In order to have great happiness you have to have great pain and unhappiness - otherwise how would you know when you're happy?"

-- Leslie Caron (1931 -)
French actress & dancer

Learning how to put positive psychology to work in our lives can be key. We can escape misery when we learn to weave every possible thread of happiness into our daily lives. We do this by selecting specific areas that we seek more of in our lives and striving daily to embrace them. This may sound odd, but sometimes to make it real we may need to take a "fake it till we make it" approach.

"You must try to generate happiness
within yourself.
If you aren't happy in one place,
chances are you won't be happy anyplace."

-- Ernie Banks (1931 – 2015)
American professional baseball shortstop

Some areas we choose might include enthusiasm or radiance, compassion or gratitude, affection or friendliness. We can learn to avoid being fussy or letting a foul temper control our moods or days. We can decide to be cheerful and upbeat, rather than miserable and negative. Actively choosing our happiness factors may sound impossibly crazy, but in this case, it's worth thinking outside the box. Sometimes we have to think a little bit crazy to get a whole lot of happiness.

*"Sanity and happiness
are an impossible combination."*

-- Mark Twain (pen name for
Samuel Langhorne Clemens) (1835 - 1910)
American writer & humorist

We have a great deal of power over our happiness. Choosing consistently positive responses and claiming optimism over pessimism helps turn the elusive into the obtainable.

*"Try to make at least one person happy
every day.
If you cannot do a kind deed, speak a kind word.
If you cannot speak a kind word,
think a kind thought.
Count up, if you can,
the treasure of happiness
that you would dispense in a week, in a year,
in a lifetime!"*

-- Lawrence G. Lovasik (1913 – 1986)
American Catholic priest & missionary

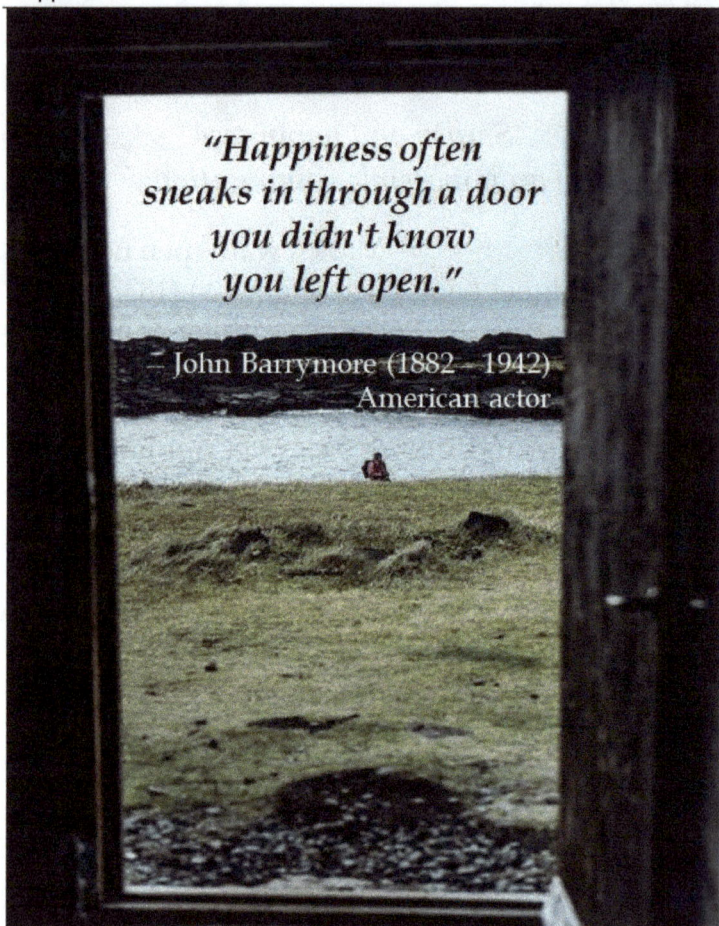

"*Happiness often sneaks in through a door you didn't know you left open.*"

– John Barrymore (1882 – 1942)
American actor

(Photo by Alexander Milo)

6

Long-Term or Temporary

Because happiness is subjective, we approach how we see it quite differently from one another. The same is true for how we describe and understand long-term versus temporary happiness.

Some say, quite simply, that happiness is long-term and pleasure is temporary. Others draw distinctions between life satisfaction and superficial hedonism. Perhaps happiness is both the positive attitude toward our life as a whole and a balance of pleasant over unpleasant incidents.

"Happiness must be cultivated. It is like character. It is not a thing to be safely let alone for a moment, or it will run to weeds."

-- Elizabeth Stuart Phelps Ward (1844 – 1911)
American author & intellectual

We all enjoy the temporary events that fill us with glee. However, we all also want a higher quality of life and sense of well-being that lasts for years and fulfills us. The search for both temporary and long-lasting happiness takes place in every corner of the world.

*"It's pretty hard to tell what
does bring happiness;
poverty and wealth have both failed."*

-- Kin Hubbard (1868 – 1930)
American cartoonist & humorist

We often seek true happiness even more diligently than material goods or monetary wealth. For some of us, finding lasting happiness is second, perhaps, only to getting into heaven,

So, we know that bouncing from one joyful pleasantry to another does not result in finding true happiness. Tidbits of pleasure do not translate into volumes of happiness.

"Everything has its wonders,
even darkness and silence,
and I learn,
whatever state I may be in,
therein to be content."

-- Helen Keller (1880 – 1968)
American author & disability rights advocate

(Photo by Gary Fultz)

In fact, we typically need times of great angst and even sadness to understand and better experience happiness. This correlates to the logic that cold, wintery weather helps us appreciate Spring all the more.

(Photo by George Cee)

When I spent Winters in southwest Florida, the weather was awesome, so Spring did not bring a noticeable contrast. When we have something to compare, we gain deeper understanding.

Other factors also influence our level of happiness. These components could include achievements, friendships, marital or relationship status, and other life circumstances.

"There are people who can do all fine and heroic things but one - keep from telling their happiness to the unhappy."

-- Mark Twain (pen name for
Samuel Langhorne Clemens) (1835 - 1910)
American writer & humorist

(Photo by Kateryna Hliznitsova)

Believe it or not, we do have control over a great deal of our happiness. The more we involve ourselves in wonderful activities, engage with positive people, and seek purposes that are beyond ourselves, the happier we become. Building greater satisfaction in Life increases true happiness. Even the process... the actual pursuit of positive, optimistic endeavors... promotes our well-being.

(Photo by Elaine Casap)

"All who joy would win must share it.
Happiness was born a Twin."

-- Lord Byron (1788 – 1824)
English poet

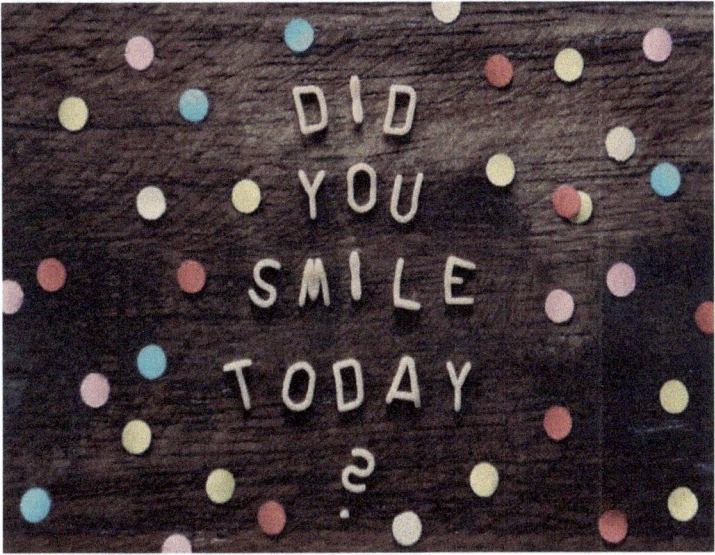

Happiness is supported every time we experience positive emotions, like joy, contentment, humor, gratitude, calm, serenity, awe, compassion, and satisfaction. We feel happiness when we feel connected to special people in our lives. Happiness is always strengthened when we take part in meaningful activities or feel a sense of purpose.

"The foolish man seeks happiness in the distance, the wise grows it under his feet."

-- James Oppenheim (1882 - 1932)
American poet & novelist

We need not worry when happiness seems to be short-lived or fleeting. Happiness can come in brief spurts. Happiness can also become a more enduring experience. The happier we can become in short spurts, the happier we can become in the long run, too.

(Photo by A. C. Taaw)

7

Happy People's Secrets

Research suggests that happy people tend to rank high on eudaimonic life satisfaction. They also score better than average on their hedonic life satisfaction.

People who are positively connected to others tend to be much happier than loners. That is not to say that we cannot be happy when we are alone. We can. But close ties with optimistic people help us to be happier ourselves.

"Your successes and happiness are forgiven only if you generously consent to share them."

-- Albert Camus (1913 – 1960)
French philosopher & author

(Photo by Pascal Bullan)

Learning the secrets or signs of a happy person can help each one of us to become happier people ourselves. When we think about the happiest people we know, we will observe some commonalities or tendencies. These are happiness secrets that we can capture for ourselves.

Here are a few secrets to being a happy person:

- Find joy in positive, long-term, and healthy relationships.
- Smile easily.
- Laugh often.
- Prioritize fun.

"The happiest people seem to be those who have no particular cause for being happy except that they are so."

-- William Inge (1913 – 1973)
American playwright & novelist

- Go with the flow; take life as it comes more easily than some.
- Live with a sense of purpose.
- Work toward goals.
- Connect genuinely with others.
- Exhibit an attitude of gratitude.
- Live by a solid set of values.

(Photo by Danie Franco)

"I am determined to be cheerful and happy in whatever situation I may find myself. For I have learned that the greater part of our misery or unhappiness is determined not by our circumstance but by our disposition."

-- Martha Washington (1731 – 1802)
American; inaugural First Lady of the U.S.

(Photo by Anita Austrika)

- Feel that living a good life is possible or happening.
- Do not play games with other people's lives or hearts.
- Exude patience and calmness.
- Do favors for others without being asked.

(Photo by S. Klimkin)

- Be self-reliant.
- Focus on personal growth.
- Find ways to give back or pay it forward.
- Open mind to new ideas, thoughts, experiences, and approaches.
- Grant others tolerance and respect, even when not reciprocated.
- Appreciate simple pleasures in life.

"One of the secrets of a happy life
is continuous small treats."

-- Iris Murdoch (1919 - 1999)
Irish novelist & philosopher

- Express more positive than negative, more optimistic than pessimistic.
- Lack captivation with material goods.
- Do not feel entitled to receive success.
- Feel accomplished or in the process of accomplishing.
- Seek answers and solutions from within.

"The secret to happiness is freedom... And the secret to freedom is courage."

-- Thucydides (c 460 BC – c 400 BC)
Athenian historian & general

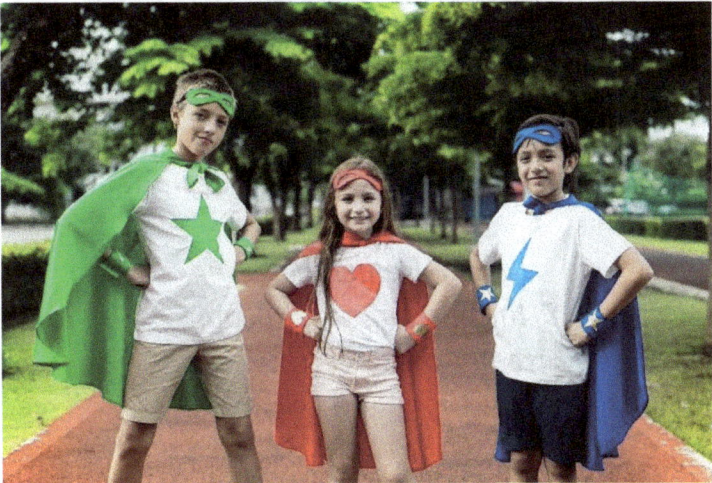

- Hold fewer expectations of others.
- Do not react to petty annoyances.

- Remain curious.
- Do not play the martyr or victim card.
- Treat others kindly.
- Practice compassion.
- Allow other people to be imperfect.
- Stay active.

- Express genuine happiness for other people and their successes.
- Practice humility, humbleness, or modesty.
- Pay attention.
- Choose not to be spiteful or insulting.

*"Remember
that the happiest people
are not those getting more,
but those giving more."*

-- H. Jackson Brown, Jr. (1940 – 2021)
American Author

- Give and receive graciously.
- Share happiness and joy openly and readily.
- Don't squash other people's happiness.
- Do not dwell on past challenges and hurts.
- Forgive and do not hold grudges.

*"There is only one way to happiness
and that is to cease
worrying about things
which are beyond the power of our will."*

-- Epictetus (50 AD – 135 AD)
Ancient Greek Stoic philosopher

- Do not anxiously worry about tomorrow.
- Exercise mental, physical, emotional, and spiritual self-care.
- Live with purposeful meaning.
- Dare to dream new dreams.

There are plenty more secrets, too. We need not gain proficiency in all of them, but the better we get at a few, the happier we will be.

"It is not how much we have,
but how much we enjoy,
that makes happiness."

-- Charles H. Spurgeon (1834 – 1892)
English Baptist preacher

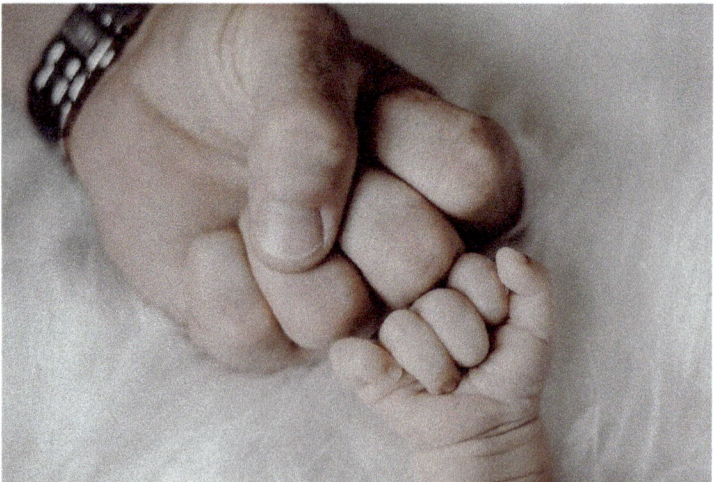

8

Developing Harmony

Sometimes we may find ourselves questioning whether or not Life is fulfilling our needs? Do we feel satisfied? Do we feel fulfilled?

We all want to experience inner peace. There may be activities we can undertake that help us feel an inner harmony and calmness that help us take on the days activities with more confidence and zeal.

We can also adapt behaviors that help us develop harmony with others around us. This may include family members or co-workers.

"He who lives in harmony with himself lives in harmony with the universe."

-- Marcus Aurelius (121 - 180 AD)
Roman Emperor & Stoic philosopher

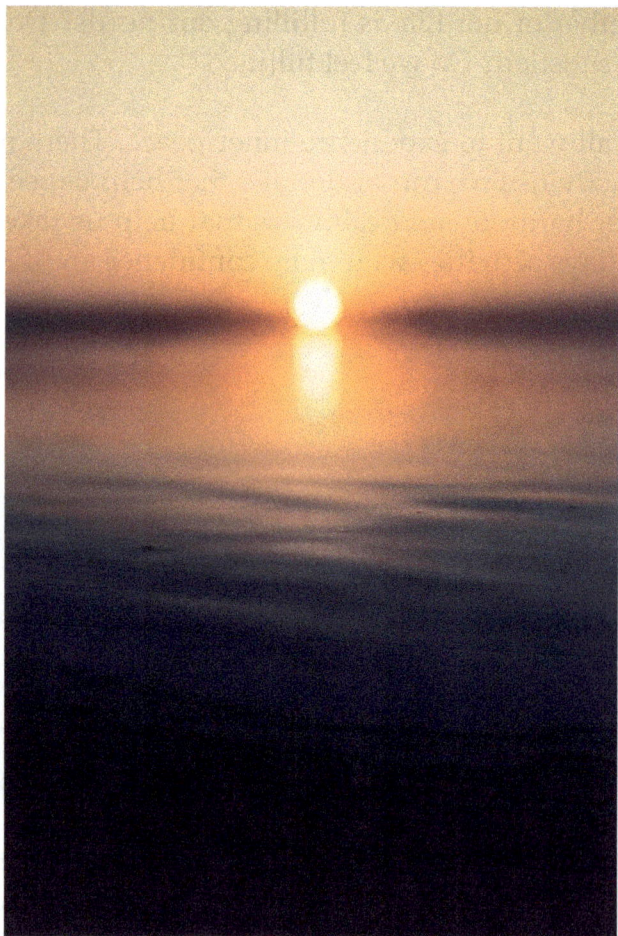

(Photo by Ameen Fahmy)

Even our most marvelous moments of merriment feel better when they give meaning to our lives. We also feel more positive when we find we can give meaning to the lives of others.

Practice makes perfect, but we want to know that we are practicing the skills that will make us happier on a daily basis. Further, developing these skills makes us happier on a long-term basis.

Another tip that may be helpful has to do with our perception of other people. We should not presume that a happy person is naturally happy. On the other hand, when we train ourselves to be happy, our happiness becomes second nature. It seems natural, as if it was always a central part of who we are.

(Photo by Tim Mossholder)

When we prioritize self-reflection, we learn about ourselves, our needs, our strengths, and our vulnerabilities. By learning about ourselves, we can also recognize where and when we need to set healthy boundaries and where to nurture our relationships.

"No person, no place, and no thing
has any power over us,
for 'we' are the only thinkers in our mind.
When we create peace and harmony
and balance in our minds,
we will find it in our lives."

-- Louise L. Hay (1926 – 2017)
American author

(Photo by Poodar Chu)

Most of us benefit by learning to say, "No." We often take on too much. Initially, we enjoy the activities or challenges, but they can start to feel oppressive, which immediately or gradually warps our sense of harmony. Moderation is key.

Managing stress is vital. We all face various levels. Inner turmoil weakens our immune system, so we need to focus on calmness. Not everything on a scale of 1 to 10 is a 10, never mind a 12 or 15.

Staying calm in stressful situations is a worthy skill. By doing so, we are exhibiting emotional stability and strength.

*"The simplification of life is
one of the steps to inner peace.
A persistent simplification
will create an inner and outer well-being
that places harmony in one's life."*

-- Peace Pilgrim (1908 – 1981)
(born Mildred Lisette Norman)
American spiritual teacher & author

We also fare better when we do not let other people's negative expressions, criticisms, and attitudes make us like them. Negativity is even more contagious than positivity. When someone else jumps on a destructive path or negative bandwagon, stand back. We need not join them.

(Photo by Louis Hansel)

Instead, we can develop and practice positive people skills. These help us develop our own inner harmony, but they also positively boost our relationship harmony.

*"But what is happiness
except the simple harmony
between a man and the life he leads?"*

-- Albert Camus (1913 – 1960)
French philosopher & author

These healthy practices include focusing on communication. Our skills are honed when we avoid being judgmental of others, gently state our thoughts, and present with positive tonality.

If we have wronged someone, everyone wins when we own up to our error. We also grow when we apologize sincerely.

Practicing mindfulness increases our harmony. Self-awareness can also help us to practice what we preach. No one is impressed when someone rants about how people should behave, while personally following a very different path.

*"Our constitution is a ray of hope:
H for harmony, O for Opportunity,
P for people's participation and E for equality."*

-- Narendra Modi (1950 -)
Indian politician
Prime Minister of India

Another great practice is showing gratitude. There are always a number of things for which we could and should be grateful. We help balance negatives in our lives when we learn to practice an attitude of gratitude.

We grow when we let people know what we most value in them. Sometimes we have to look very closely, but it's worthwhile to seek and find the positives in ourselves and other people.

Introspection is healthy. We all have psychological needs. Accepting and understanding this fact helps us better meet our needs. We can then focus on our growth and balance. We can find our "happy place."

"Happiness is not a matter of intensity but of balance, order, rhythm and harmony."

-- Thomas Merton (1915 – 1968)
American Trappist monk & writer

We are finding harmony. We are building and supporting our harmony... that sense of balance and personal growth that builds long-lasting happiness.

"With an eye made quiet
by the power of harmony,
and the deep power of joy,
we see into the life of things."

-- William Wordsworth (1770 – 1850)
English poet

(Photo by Juli Kosolapova)

9

In Closing

Exactly how much control do we have over our happiness? This can depend on how we are letting ourselves be guided in Life.

"The most worthwhile thing is to try to put happiness into the lives of others."

-- Robert Baden-Powell (1857 – 1941)
British Army officer & founder of the
Boy Scouts Association

Some people are inner directed. They follow their own values. They do not let any outside forces determine what is meaningful to them. They can be happy without external entertainment.

"Thousands of candles
can be lighted from a single candle,
and the life of the candle will not be shortened.
Happiness never decreases by being shared."

-- Buddha (c 563 or 480 BC – c 483 or 400 BC)
(Siddhartha Gautama)
Founder of Buddhism

(Photo by Mike Labrum)

"Do not speak of your happiness to one less fortunate than yourself."

-- Plutarch (40 – 120 AD)
Greek Platonist philosopher

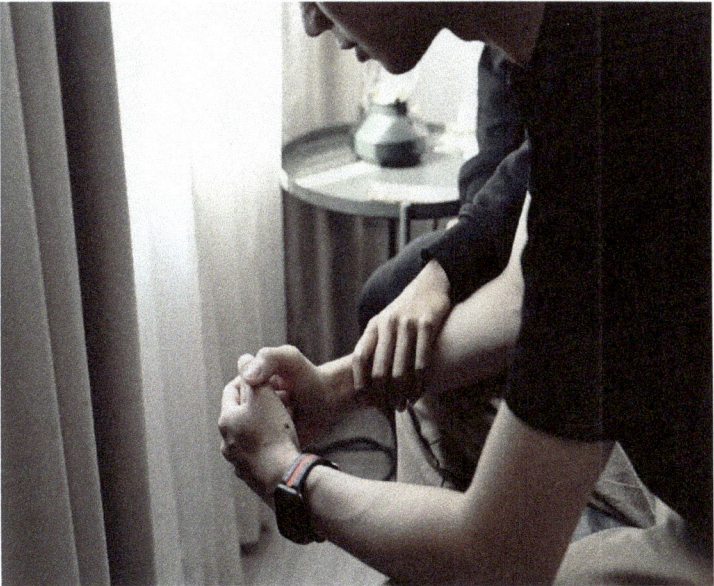

Some people are outer directed. They need stimulation from other people and places and events. They tend to become easily bored when left alone.

(Photo by Priscilla DuPreez)

"God will prepare everything for our perfect happiness in heaven, and if it takes my dog being there, I believe he'll be there."

-- Billy Graham (1918 – 2018)
American evangelist, civil rights advocate &
Southern Baptist minister

To be happy, we need to feel good physically, mentally, socially, spiritually, and emotionally. We also need to understand that happiness comes from within us. We can be happier based on what we choose to think, feel, and do.

"Friends show their love in times of trouble, not in happiness."

-- Euripides (c 480 BC – c 406 BC)
Greek tragedian

(Photo by Helena Lopes)

We need not let our circumstances determine our happiness and meaningfulness in Life. We can put ourselves in the driver's seat and follow a path to a life of greater happiness and well-being.

"Even if happiness forgets you a little bit, never completely forget about it."

-- Jaques Prévert (1900 - 1977)
French poet & screenwriter

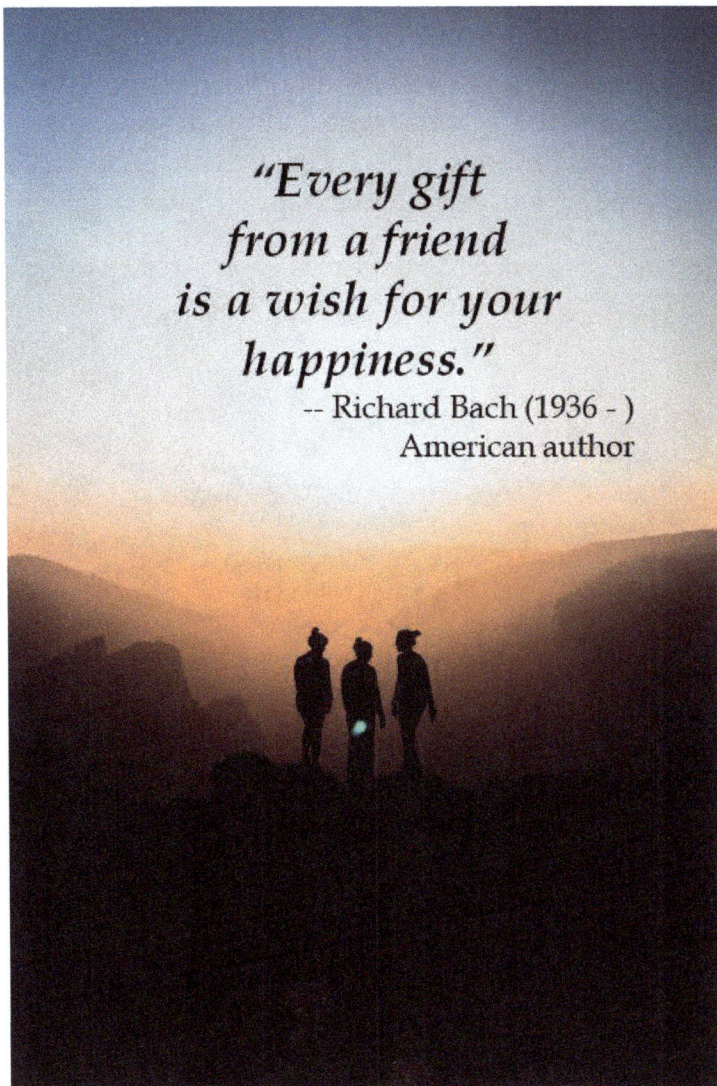

"*Every gift
from a friend
is a wish for your
happiness.*"
-- Richard Bach (1936 -)
American author

(Photo by Karl Magnuson)

We will face difficult crossroads and hardships, but we can choose how to respond to each one. Those personal choices can make all the difference… the positive difference. Let's break free from the obstacles that may be blocking our happiness. We each have the power to be happy despite stress, challenges, and circumstances. When we learn to cope better, we learn to live happier lives.

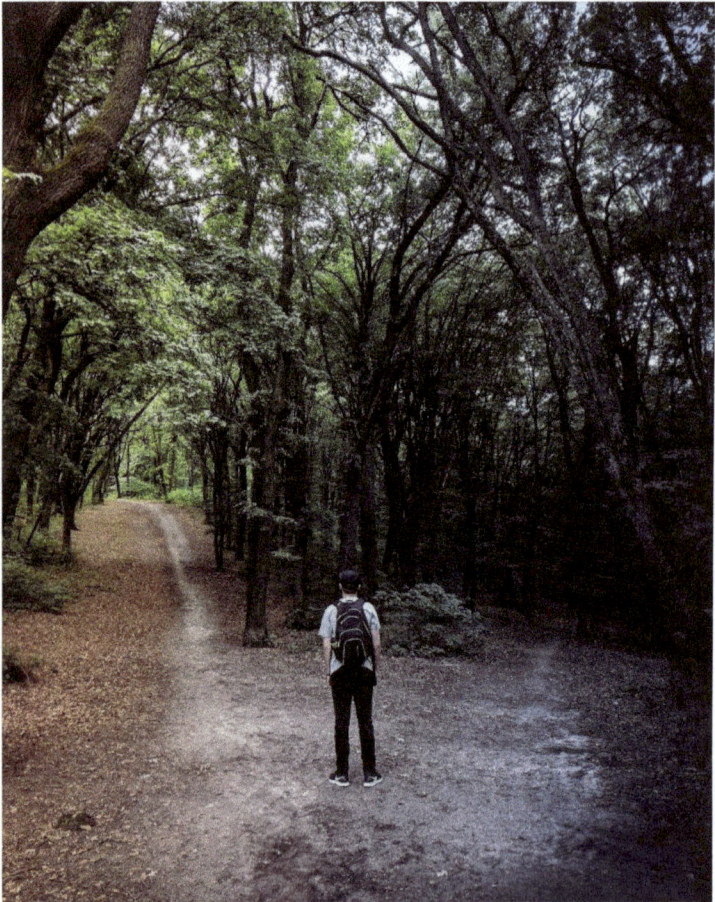

(Photo by Vladislav Babienko)

Photography Credits

Thank you to everyone who entrusted me with the use of their beautiful photographs.

Mark Adriane
Melissa Askew
Anita Austvika
Vladislav Babienko
Szilvia Basso
Herbert Bieser
Andrew Bui
Pascal Bullan
Elaine Casap
George Cee
Poodar Chu
Mateus Campos Felipe
Priscilla DuPreez
Kenny Eliason
Ameen Fahmy
Osman Firat
Danie Franco
Gary Fultz
John Godinez
Caju Gomes
Louis Hansel
Taylor Heery
Kateryna Hliznitsova
Tran Huynh

S. Klimkin
Juli Kosolapova
Ahmet Kurt
Mike Labrum
Helena Lopes
Kyle Loftus
Karl Magnuson
Davaiah Mallang
Alexander Milo
Ricardo Moura
Tim Mossholder
Elena Mozhvilo
Aizhan Okisheva
Mi Pham
Stephame Pratt
Greg Rakozy
Aleksandra
    Sapozhnikova
Daria Shatova
Noah Sillimann
A.C. Taaw
Luca Upper
Dimitris Vetsikas
Suzanna D. Williams

Special thanks to Aaron Burden
for the cover photo.

(Photo by Aaron Burden)

About the Author

Cathy Burnham Martin's first published work came in elementary school when an early poem won a town library contest. That was back when her parents refused to let her have the then-popular "Chatty Cathy" doll, stating that one chatty Cathy in the house was more than enough. Though poetry took a back seat, she drove her writing and blabbing proficiencies along a highly eclectic career path through college recruitment, telecom marketing, corporate communications, TV broadcasting with an ABC affiliate, station management of an award-winning PEG-access station, bank organizing, and investor relations. An active board member and volunteer, she received Easter Seals' David P. Goodwin Lifetime Commitment Award. This professional voiceover artist, humorist, musical actress, journalist, and dedicated foodie earned numerous awards as a news anchor and businesswoman. She has produced and hosted groundbreaking documentaries, TV specials, and news reports, from the Moscow Superpower Summit and the opening of the Berlin Wall to coverage of Presidential Primaries. A born storyteller and business speaker dubbed "The Morale Booster," Cathy is a member of Actors Equity and writes daily articles for social media and the GoodLiving123.com website.

(Photo by Pascal Bullan)

<u>Other Titles</u>

Life Seasonings series:
   Perspectives
   Hope

The Destiny trilogy:
   Destiny of Dreams… Time Is Dear
   Destiny of Determination… Faith and Family
   Destiny of Daring… Never Forget

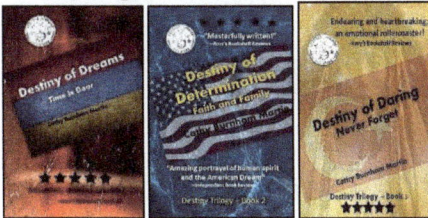

A Dangerous Book for Dogs:
   Train Your Humans with the Bandit Method
Dog Days in the Life of the Miles-Mannered Man

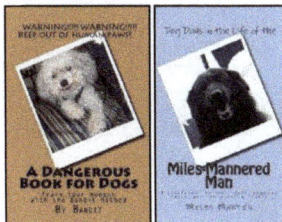

Healthy Thinking Habits:
  Seven Attitude Skills Simplified
Good Living Skills: Learned from My Mother
Encouragement: How to Be and Find Your Best

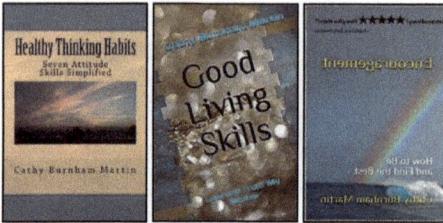

Of the Same Blood: Your Eurasian Heritage
The Ronald…
  Daydreams, Wonderments & Other Ponderings

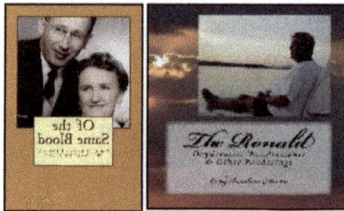

The Bimbo Has Brains… and Other Freaky Facts
The Bimbo Has MORE Brains…
  Surviving Political Correctness

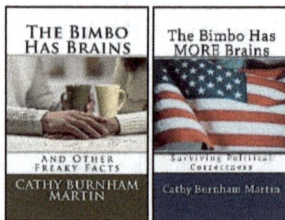

From the KISS Keep It Super Simple cookbooks:

50 Years of Fabulous Family Favorites
    Sippers, Starters, and Sweets
    Lunch, Brunch, and Entrees
    Sides, Soup, Salad, Snacks, Etc.

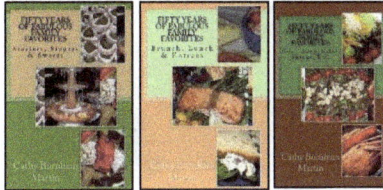

Champagne! Facts, Fizz, Food, & Fun
Cranberry Cooking

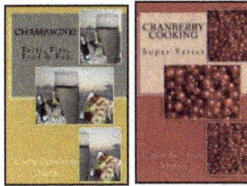

Dockside Dining: (series)
    Round One
    A Second Helping
    Back for Thirds

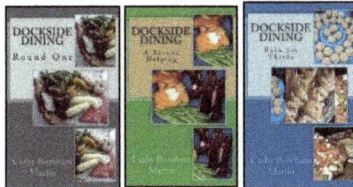

Lobacious Lobster…
Decadently Super Simple Recipes

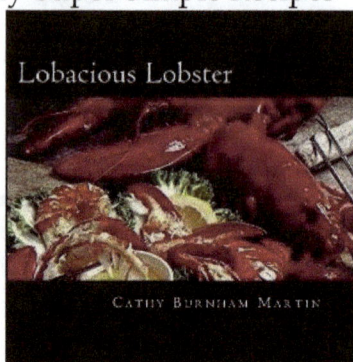

Find all books by Cathy Burnham Martin in paperback, digital, and audiobook formats anywhere books are sold and on her **www.GoodLiving123.com** site.

Partial List of Audiobooks Narrated by Cathy Burnham Martin

Fiction
Destiny Trilogy:
    Destiny of Dreams... Time Is Dear
      (Violent content warning)
    Destiny of Determination... Faith and Family
    Destiny of Daring... Never Forget
A Dangerous Book for Dogs...
    Train Your Humans with the Bandit Method
Kremlins Trilogy (Violent content warning)
    Citadels of Fire
    Bastions of Blood
    Dungeons of Destiny:
        An Epic Russian Historical Romance
Daniel's Fork: A Mystery Set in the
        Daniel's Fork Universe
          (Adult content warning)
The Relentless Brit

Non-Fiction
Encouragement: How to Be and Find the Best
Good Living Skills... Learned from My Mother
Healthy Thinking Habits:
      Seven Attitude Skills Simplified
The Bimbo Has Brains: And Other Freaky Facts
The Bimbo Has MORE Brains:
      Surviving Political Correctness
31 Days to a Stronger Marriage:
      A Guide to Building Closer Relationships
Exploring Past Lives: A Guide to the Soul's Travels
Why We Fail in Love: A Study into the Pursuit of
      One of Mankind's Most Precious Desires
The Hormone Fix: Naturally Rebalance Your System
    in 10 Weeks

www.ingramcontent.com/pod-product-compliance
Lightning Source LLC
Chambersburg PA
CBHW060401050426
42449CB00009B/1839